Trade on the
TAOS MOUNTAIN TRAIL

Deborah Martinez Martinez, Ph.D.

Illustrated by Robert W. Pacheco

Books available for classroom use for $5 @.
www.vanishinghorizons.com: scavenger
pages, math pages, printable maps. Call
719-561-0993 or 719-544-4040 or email
vanishinghorizons1@me.com

VANISHING
HORIZONS
PUBLISHING THE PAST FOR THE FUTURE

Pueblo, Colorado

2010

INTRODUCTION

Trade on the American Frontier

Trading is the buying or selling of goods or services. Historically trade did not always involve money. The trade goods have changed over time but the idea of trade is the same from the caveman to today's Wall Street stock traders. One person has what the other person wants. In order to get what is wanted, the two parties exchange goods or services.

• Trade on the American frontier was conducted between the various Native American Nations and the Americans, the French/English/Canadians, and the Spanish/Mexican without the use of money.

• Why should you care about this trading? Because your family, your ancestors, were involved and may still have some of the trade goods as heirlooms.

• Modern borders cannot limit the story of trade. People traded from the far north in Canada, across the United States of America and into the United States of Mexico. Traders came from China, Russia, Greenland and Iceland.

• How do we know about the history of trade? Because anthropologists find goods made by one group in far away archaeological excavations of other people. Abalone shells from southern California were found in central Mexico and Ohio.

• Think about the frontier as only four grandmothers ago (200 years) when Colorado and Wyoming were part of the Louisiana Purchase and New Mexico was on the northern frontier of the new country of Mexico.

• In this book, we are going to show how the Taos Mountain Trail connected the trade centers of the Taos Pueblo and the village of Taos to El Pueblo Trading Post and Bent's Old Fort on the Arkansas River. These locations are National Historic Sites.

Although the focus is on Colorado and New Mexico, we will begin with the original inhabitants of the region – the Native American Nations – and their trade routes. The Spanish and French followed the ancient trade routes created by the Native Americans. The fur trappers and traders used the same trails. Modern highways sometimes follow these old trade routes.

Deborah Martens Martinez

CONTENTS

What Was Trade for the Native Americans?

Native American nations supported a wide network of trade. People used the rivers as roads to travel and trade. They traveled from Hudson Bay, Canada, to Central America and from the Atlantic to the Pacific. A carved pipe from the Missouri red pipestone quarry could be traded from hand to hand before reaching people in California.

Macaw feathers from central Mexico were found in the excavations of the Cahokian mound builder in central Missouri. Some of these trade centers were located near or on major rivers: the Mississippi, Columbia, and Ohio Rivers in the east; north to Saskatchewan and Missouri Rivers; the Arkansas, Red and Rio Grande Rivers in the southwestern region. The Zuni and Taos Pueblos served as trade centers as did the Chaco Canyon area.

Photo Denver Public Library

With dogs to haul goods using a *travois* (long poles attached to the sides of the animal), a family could travel six miles a day. After the Spanish introduced the horse to the Americas, the people could travel 15 miles a day.

Photo Denver Public Library

Trading Horses

Having horses changed the life of the Native Americans. They could travel over a wider area. Hunting buffalo became easier. Some tribes, such as the Nez Perce, became known for horse breeding.

There were traders and trading cultures. The word "Arapaho" means "trader" in the Pawnee language. Since traders came from far away, the goods had to be small and portable. An example of a widely traded item is the bead. Beads were made of polished bone, shells, carved soft rocks, turquoise, pearls or other precious or semi-precious stones.

Other small items, like herbs, dyes, porcupine quills and feathers were easy to carry. Hides, furs, pottery, woven fabric of cotton, yucca, or other fibers were all part of the great trading network. The copper workers of the eastern United Sta[tes] produced copper blades, beads, bangles and small tools as trade goods.

THE BUFFALO PROVIDES THE GOOD LIFE...

Robes for warmth

Brains, Liver for tanning

Foretop spun into rope

Horns for cups

Horns for gunpowder

Tongue is specialty meat

Bladder is water bag

Bones for tools

Bone marrow is 'prairie butter'

Sinew is sewing thread

Hump is specialty meat

Hard fat is tallow for candles

Stomach paunch is cooking pot

Meat for jerky

Intestines to stuff with meat

Bile for seasoning

Tail is a flyswatter

Droppings for fuel

Nose for specialty meat

Hooves make rattles or glue

2000 pound buffalo = 600 pounds of meat
10 buffalo robes = 1 Navajo blanket
20 buffalo hides = 1 teepee

Sign Language

Traders used sign language instead of a common vocal language to communicate. With nearly 500 Native American nations and 390 languages, there was a need for sign language. The hand gestures were numerous and could describe detailed information. The American sign system used by modern hearing impaired people evolved from this early communication method.

One Buffalo Robe =
3 Metal Knives
1 Large Kettle
36 Iron Arrowheads
1/2 Yard of Calico

Beaver Trapped to Near Extinction

For 200 years, European men's top hats were made of beaver hide. A dried beaver hide was called "made beaver" and was used as money in trade.

3

NATIVE AMERICAN TRADE ROUTES

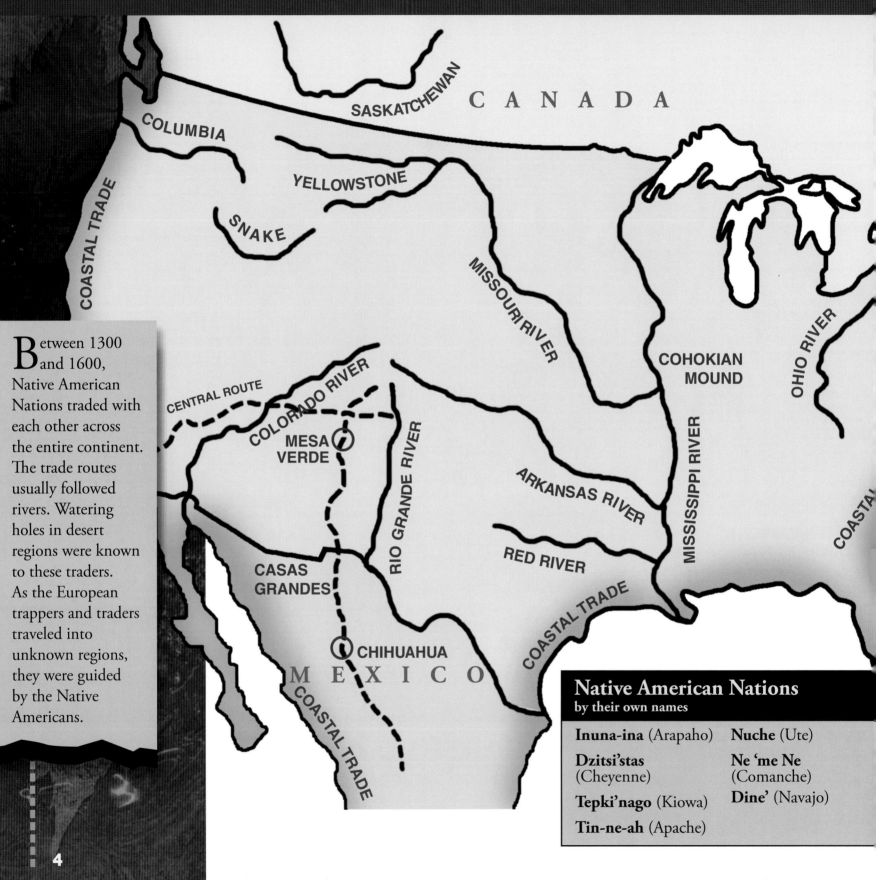

Between 1300 and 1600, Native American Nations traded with each other across the entire continent. The trade routes usually followed rivers. Watering holes in desert regions were known to these traders. As the European trappers and traders traveled into unknown regions, they were guided by the Native Americans.

COASTAL TRADE

COLUMBIA

SASKATCHEWAN

CANADA

YELLOWSTONE

SNAKE

MISSOURI RIVER

CENTRAL ROUTE

COLORADO RIVER

MESA VERDE

RIO GRANDE RIVER

COHOKIAN MOUND

OHIO RIVER

ARKANSAS RIVER

MISSISSIPPI RIVER

RED RIVER

COASTAL

CASAS GRANDES

COASTAL TRADE

CHIHUAHUA

MEXICO

COASTAL TRADE

Native American Nations
by their own names

Inuna-ina (Arapaho)	**Nuche** (Ute)
Dzitsi'stas (Cheyenne)	**Ne 'me Ne** (Comanche)
Tepki'nago (Kiowa)	**Dine'** (Navajo)
Tin-ne-ah (Apache)	

Coastal Routes

Coastal regions provided north/south highways on both the Atlantic and Pacific coasts. The Gulf coast was a trade route into South America. Abalone shells from Southern California as well as dried salmon and whale oil from the northern coast were traded to the east. The Caddo people of the South traded hardwoods for bow making to groups farther west.

Rio Grande River

Traders traveled between Mesa Verde (CO) and Casas Grandes (Northern Mexico). The Rio Grande River guided travelers north and south and connected with the Gulf Coastal trail. The twelve pueblos of New Mexico used this route for trade with the Tarahumara and Yaquis in northern Mexico.

Columbia River

In the northwest, the Columbia, Yellowstone and Snake Rivers helped to move obsidian—a shiny black stone formed in volcanos—from the west to those farther east and south. The Crow, Assiniboin of Canada, and Blackfoot traded in this area. The Columbia also connected the northwest to the central plains via the Missouri.

Yellowstone River

Traders followed the rough shores of the Yellowstone River through the mountain valleys. The route was probably used by the Native Americans of the Saskatchewan regions in Canada to come and trade with the Nez Perce, Blackfoot and Crow.

The Missouri River

The long and wide Missouri River started in North Dakota. It flowed south and east to connect with the Mississippi River. The Mandan, Hidatsa, and Arikara people traded buffalo hides, food and flints along this river.

Mississippi River

The Mississippi River's headwaters are in the Great Lakes. It meets the Missouri River near the Cohokian Mound people's territory (near St. Louis, MO). The Cohokian city of 20,000 people was larger than any European city of the time. They traded copper tools to central and northern Canada.

Ohio River

The Ohio, Tennessee and Big Sandy Rivers cross through the eastern states, joining tribes from throughout the region. Traveling traders were common and welcome among the Ottawa, Shawnee, and Micmac villages.

Central Route

An overland route through New Mexico to Colorado and across the southern tip of Nevada reached Los Angeles. The route was used continuously for over 1000 years and followed the Colorado River in part. The route became the Old Spanish Trail.

TRADE GOODS

Trade Goods of the First Nations

Sea shells—dentalium, abalone • Bright colored feathers • Buffalo horn cups, spoons • Seal or walrus ivory • Red or yellow ochre (for paint) • Blue beads • Obsidian for knives, spear points • Hickory branches for bows • Pipestone for pipes • Porcupine quills for decoration • Tobacco Knickanick • Woven blankets • Pottery of pueblos • Nuts or dried berries of the region • Pecans from south • Walnuts from the northeast • Piñon from the southwest • Buffalo robes • Dried vegetables: Corn, Squash, beans, prickly pear • Dried fruits: prickly pear, gooseberry, chokecherry, currents • Pine or juniper pitch • Lichens for dye • Dried meats, jerky • Healing herbs: ocha, mints, aspen bark, wild four o'clocks • Yucca cordage • Horse hair ropes • Captives of other tribes • Unique seeds or seedpods as beads • Gourds for carrying water • Eagle feathers

Robert W. Pacheco

The Native Americans used the resources of the area for their survival and for trading with others. The animals of the region—deer, elk, buffalo and bear—provided furs for warmth, hides for leather and housing, and meat for food. Everything the Native Americans needed, their environment provided.

Hides of wolves, beaver, mountain lion, lynx, otter, marten, and ermine provided many resources. Bear claws, and elk teeth were used in decoration. Wearing the hide of a certain animal that was difficult to capture, such as a badger, showed bravery and cleverness. A full-grown badger or mountain lion could attack and kill a man.

Douglas Candelaria

Captives

Captives of other tribes were also traded. If a servant was wanted, someone might trade several items or a horse for a child or woman. The more hands a household had, the more labor could be accomplished. One woman could tan about ten hides each season. More workers allowed the family group to gain wealth by having more goods to trade.

Some captives were treated badly. Sometimes a captive might marry and become part of the tribe. Child captives might be adopted into the tribe. Also, captives were valuable for their knowledge. A captive's knowledge of different healing methods, multiple languages, new trade routes, or new techniques was valued. In this way, technology was transferred from nation to nation.

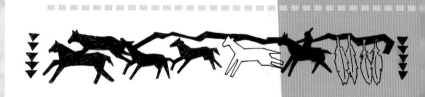

Boys learned how to handle a bow by age four

European trappers and traders traveled across the county following already established trade routes of the Native Americans. They used sign language to communicate.

Before the trading session, a series of small sticks were laid out. The trader would indicate, by the number of sticks, how many of an item would be bartered for another.

Following the trading, there would be feasting, games and then dancing. Games such as shinny ball, a type of field hockey, and lacrosse lasted for hours. Guessing games or games of skill might include betting on the outcome.

Douglas Candelaria

Trade Goods: Center: Painted buffalo robe. From left to right: Horses, *parfleche*—a decorated container, doll with red stroud leggings and real hair, and dried corn.

Denver Public Library

European Trade Goods

Red stroud cloth	Buttons of bone, shell
Striped cloth	Bells
Black silk	Small mirrors
Indian calico	Whiskey
Ivory combs	Trade Blankets
Metal awls	Rifles, muskets
Needles: small and large	Lead for ammunition
Red flannel	Gunpowder
Vermillion dye powder	Knives all types
Glass beads of different colors	
Gun flints	
Gun worms	
Buttons of glass, marble	

At the end of the 1700s, the villages of the Mandan, Hidatsa and Arikara hosted trade fairs that included the Plains Indians on the Missouri River. When the Europeans came to trade, they accepted horses, furs, and hides in exchange for guns and manufactured goods such as blankets, vermillion, and glass beads.

There were many trading companies such as the Hudson Bay Trade Company in Canada, its rival the North West Company, Pacific Fur Company, John Jacob Astor's American Fur Company, Spaniard Manual Lisa's Lisa, Menard, and Morrison Fur Company and the Missouri Fur Company.

In 1790, the government passed a series of laws meant to protect the Native Americans during trade. The laws, called the Trade and Intercourse Acts, failed.

At the mountain man rendezvous, or gatherings, the companies distributed goods to their traders and collected the beaver pelts and other hides. From 1783 on, the North West Company met at Grand Portage and later at Fort William.

1300-2010

The Taos Pueblo people began building their home between 1300 and 1450. The Rio Grande River ran nearby and the Taos Valley had land to grow crops for food and for trade. The Taos Pueblo is built of *adobe* and is five stories high with ladders to reach the rooms on the upper floors. In the earliest days of the Pueblo, the ground floors had no windows or doors and were entered through the roof.

Robert W. Pacheco

Taos and Picuris Pueblos were leading trading centers where Native American traders gathered. Taos and Pecos were accessible from both the Rocky Mountains and the Great Plains. Fairs were held annually in July and August attracting Navajos, Utes, Arapahos, Pawnees and Comanches.

Douglas Candelaria

Trade goods in 1786 were reported to include hides, captives, meat, horses and guns. Comanches traded more than 600 hides, meat and tallow alone. French, New Mexican, and American traders came for t events. Chihuahuano traders brought imported goods. The Taos Pue was a trade center because of its location at the center of this lush val Taos Pueblo trade items, such as pottery for cooking and baskets, hav been found in far away locations.

Taos people were farmers. They irrigated their fields working together in family or clan groups. They grew beans, squash, and corn together in the same fields. These vegetables, both fresh and dried, were the mainstay of their trade along with tobacco, cotton, and melons. *Metates* of stone were used to grind corn and other grains.

Clockwise from top: Vermillion, porcupine quills, medicine bag with bead and quill work, abalone shell, goose wing fan.

Douglas S. Candelaria

No fighting was allowed at the trade fair. Often enemy groups, such as the Comanche and the Navajo, came to trade with the Taos people and each other. The people at Taos speak the Tiwa language but when the great trade fairs were held in the summer, the traders all used sign language to communicate.

When the Spanish came in 1598, they demanded the Pueblo people work in the Spanish homes and fields. They called it the Spanish *encomiendo* system. For the pueblos, it was like slavery.

In 1680, Popé, a young leader of the San Juan Pueblo, led a successful revolt against the Spanish. Those Spanish who were not killed fled to Chihuahua, Mexico abandoning the settlements. In 1692, the Spanish returned promising to change their ways. The Spanish outlawed the annual Taos Pueblo trade fairs in 1780.

Taos Pueblo is on the National Registry of Historic Places and is a World Heritage Center. The Taos Sacred Blue Lake was returned to them in 1970.

Pottery was a desired trade item. Each of the many original pueblos in New Mexico had their own designs and their own locations for digging clay and mica. Mica was a fireproof mineral mixed with the clay to allow the pot to be used near fire without cracking. During trading, buffalo, elk and deer hides were laid out and bargains were made. The quality of the work was evaluated. Woven cotton cloth was valuable as a trade item.

Left to Right: Burnished redware, Ysleta Pueblo, NM, painted blackware, Casas Grandes, Mexico, woven pine needle basket, Tarahumara, Mexico.

LOS ANGELES
TAOS
SANTA FE
EL PASO
CHIHUAHUA
DURANGO
LAGO
MEXICO CITY
PUEBLA

EL CAMINO REAL

1609-1848

Los arrieros, the mule drovers, loaded and guided the mule trains for the traders. The success of a trading venture depended on the arrieros' skill in packing and caring for the mules.

Freight wagons were large and heavy with flat bottoms. Using mules, the wagons traveled about 12 miles per day.

1843 Trade Goods
(Listed by Jose Chavez)

105,00 yards of *lienzo* (linen)	1 gross of pencils
48,700 yards of *indiana* (calico)	1 dozen brushes
10,000 yards of assorted fabrics	10 dozen assorted necklaces
250 dozen scarves handkerchiefs	4 dozen ink stands
13 dozen hats	3 dozen pairs of scissors
29 dozen pair of stockings	7 dozen ivory combs
36 gross of buttons	6 boxes of ribbons
5 dozen razors	3 accordions
1 box of needles	7 silk hats
3 gross of thimbles	10 guns
10 mirrors	1 dozen muslin dresses
4 sets of pistols	6 dozen silk gloves
54 strings of beads	4 dozen silk shoes

Santa Fe to Mexico City – 1700 miles in three months

The Camino Real is a network of roads originally meant to supply the missions in northmost regions of New Spain. The roads belonged to the King of Spain and were supported by the government. Caravans traveled north from Mexico City or Chihuahua with supplies and priests. Sometimes traders used the same caravan and wagons for their goods.

One branch of the Camino Real extended from Mexico City going north to Chihuahua, across the desert lands and into Santa Fe. Another branch served the Pacific coast and transported supplies to the missions in California. The road between Santa Fe and Los Angeles began in 1829-30 under Antonio Armijo and others. It was called the Old Spanish Trail (1830-46) but was not part of the Camino Real system, as it was not supported by the government.

THE CAMINO TRADE ROUTE CONTINUED TO BE AN IMPORTANT ROAD FROM SANTA FE TO MEXICO

In 1792, Pedro Vial, a French gunsmith and Indian trader, was commissioned by New Spain to find a northern route to the United States. Vial pioneered a route from Santa Fe to St. Louis. The primary traders on the Camino Real, and later the Santa Fe Trail, were the aristocratic families of the Chavezes, Armijos, Pereas, Oteros, Yrizarris. These Mexican traders bought American and European products transporting the trade goods to New Mexico and Mexican markets. By 1843, Mexicans became the majority of merchants, wagon masters and drivers involved in the overland traffic. Traders paid taxes on goods brought into Mexico.

Efectos de pais, or local, New Mexican trade goods, included buckskins, buffalo and deer hides, piñon nuts, coarse wool cloth, *serapes*, stocking, moccasins, raw wool, and *colchas* (woolen blankets). Herds of sheep, some as large as several thousand, were taken to Mexico to be sold.

In 1841, Señor Antonio José Chávez departed Independence, Missouri, with 30 wagons carrying 72 tons of merchandise.

Although large freight wagons were used for long distances, the two-wheeled *carretas* were used for narrow, mountain passes and shorter distances. Carretas could be small and drawn by one mule or large enough to need a yoke (two) of oxen.

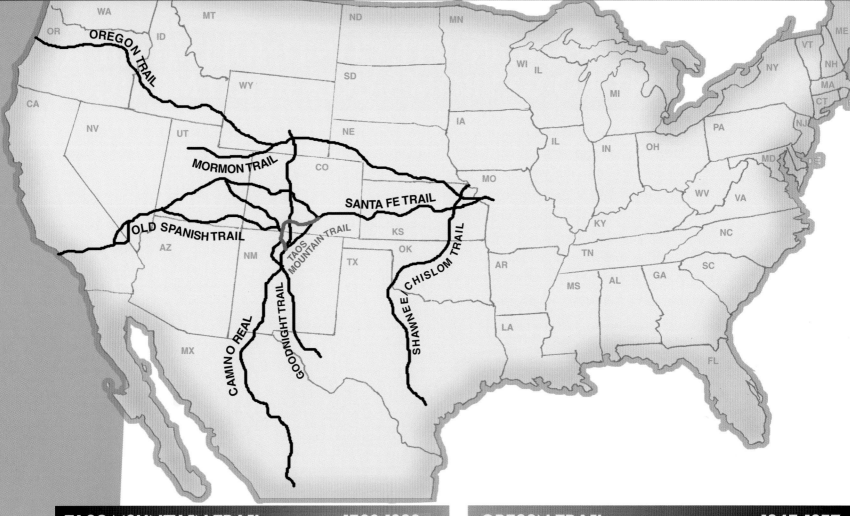

TAOS MOUNTAIN TRAIL • • • • • • 1300-1880

The Taos Mountain Trail was continuously used by Native Americans, fur trappers, and traders going back and forth over the Sangre de Cristo Mountains with mules or horses. The trail was too small for freight wagon traffic but was important as a quick route linking the Arkansas River Valley and the Taos community. Also called the Trapper's Trail.

OREGON TRAIL • • • • • • • • • • • 1843-1857

Emigrants traveling to the gold fields of northern California used this route but the Oregon Trail was important for early fur trade as well. The Oregon Trail is 2000 miles from Independence, MO, to Oregon City. Smaller freight wagons were used on this trail because of the high mountains they crossed.

GOODNIGHT TRAIL • • • • • • • • • • • 1866

The Goodnight-Loving Trail was more than 2000 miles from Texas to Wyoming. The Trail, basically a cattle drive route, was first blazed by Charles Goodnight and Oliver Loving in 1866. Goodnight delivered cattle to the Native American reservation at Fort Sumner for the army. Near Pueblo, Colorado, Goodnight built corrals and barns to hold his stock until ready to transport.

SHAWNEE & CHISLOM TRAILS • 1867-1872

The Shawnee Trail crossed Texas, Oklahoma and Kansas to take cattle to the railroad lines near Sedalia and Kansas City. The cattle were then transported by railroad east or west.

Denver Public Library

SANTA FE TRAIL • • • • • • • • • 1792-1880

In 1792, Pedro Vial mapped out the 800-mile route from Missouri and Santa Fe (NM) in New Spain. After 1821, Mexico opened overland trade. In 1825, the U. S. Congress signed a treaty with the Osage Native Americans obtaining the right of way for the Santa Fe Trail as a public highway. Large wagons, both Contestoga and freight wagons, were used to transport manufactured goods to Santa Fe and farther south into Chihuahua and Durango, Mexico.

MORMON TRAIL • • • • • • • • • • 1841-1860

The Mormon Trail followed the same route as the Oregon Trail but turned south at Fort Bridger to the Great Salt Lake Valley. By some estimates, 320,000 people traveled this route to reach Utah.

OLD SPANISH TRAIL • • • • • • • • 1830-1848

The Old Spanish Trail between Santa Fe and Los Angeles reflects an older Native American trade route, in use for nearly 1,000 years. It was not part of the Camino Real. Traders using loaded mule trains from Santa Fe took *efectos de pais* (local goods such as woolens, blankets) to California and returned with herds of horses and mules.

CAMINO REAL • • • • • • • • • • • 1680-1848

The Camino Real trade route was also called the Chihuahua Trail because so many expeditions actually left from Chihuahua, Mexico, instead of Mexico City. The journey was 1500 miles from Mexico City to Santa Fe. Caravans left Mexico City every three years to take supplies to the Santa Fe.

Spanish Settlers

Spanish settlers came to Taos Valley from New Spain when the province of New Mexcio was established in 1598. Fray Francisco de Zamora was sent to the northernmost pueblos of Taos and Picurís to live with the people to teach religion. In 1610, the Mission of San Geronimo was built. Land grants were given to individuals beginning in 1715 to settle Taos Valley, sometimes violating the land already reserved for the Taos Pueblo.

Trader Severino Martinez, his wife Maria del Carmel, and three children moved to Taos in 1802. In 1804, Severino built the Martinez *Hacienda* and enlarged it several times to make room for his extended family and servants. Plain from the outside, the hacienda was like a fortress built to protect the family from attack.

Severino ignored Spanish laws when he went north thru the Native American pathway known as the Taos Mountain Trail to trade with the bands of prairie Native Americans in Colorado. Severino also traveled down the Camino Real to sell his sheep in Mexico. At his death he owned 5000 sheep.

The church of San Francisco de Assisi in Ranchos de Taos was finished around 1815. It is designated as a World Heritage Church.

1723 Spanish government forbids trade with the French and limited trade only to Taos and Pecos. In reality, the French and the British continued to trade inside New Spain whenever they could. If caught they were imprisoned and not allowed to leave New Spain.

1776 Spanish Census listed 306 Spanish living in Taos Valley.

1780 The Annual Taos Trade Fairs were outlawed by the Spanish. Trade continued.

1795 The present town of Taos was established when 63 families were given the Don Fernando de Taos Land Grant.

FLOOR

PLAN

Children in Taos households worked more than played. These two girls are hauling water to sprinkle on the *adobe* floors or to wash clothes. They often played word games like riddles or told stories as they worked.

Each member of the Martinez *Hacienda* worked to produce goods for trade. Women made socks and clothing, wove blankets or wool fabric. Men tended to the herds of sheep, goats, mules, and horses, giving medical treatments if needed. They traveled to trade with various groups or to take supplies to shepherds in the high mountains.

Captives of the Spanish

Native American captives were purchased from other Native American nations. Sometimes they were abducted from their villages by Spanish soldiers. Since the Spanish/Mexican government did not allow slavery, the captives were called *rescates* or rescued people. Captives were taught the Catholic religion, provided clothing and food, and baptized. They were a large workforce for the Spanish. Captives taken as children often lost their native language and customs. They were not free to leave the service of the family and became *genizaros* or Native Americans without access to their own cultures.

Captured Native American men were sold to the silver mines in Mexico. This domestic slavery continued into the early years of the American administration before it became illegal in 1865.

In 1821, New Spain became Mexico gaining its independence from Spain. Mexico opened its borders to trade although licenses were required. Taxes were charged for goods coming into the country.

Taos was 40 miles north of the Spanish capital of Santa Fe. There was a customs house to gather taxes from traders in Santa Fe but not in Taos. It was easier for traders to enter and exit the country through Taos and avoid the high taxes required by Spanish law. Sometimes traders had their goods taken away if their licenses to trade were not in order. In Taos, movement of illegal goods such as whiskey and guns was less likely to reach the ears of government agents. Although Taos was not on the Santa Fe Trail, its citizens profited from the trade.

The silver coins most often used on the frontier were the Spanish or Mexican *real*. The silver or gold coins were one ounce of solid metal such as those struck in Chihuahua, marked "Ca," after Mexico's liberation from Spain.

The coin is often referred to as the Mexican or eagle dollar. Because of its reliable silver content, the U.S. Congress declared it legal tender.

When change was needed, the coin was cut into eight pieces or bits, by a blacksmith. Two bits of the eight real coin was one quarter. Coins of other countries were also used, when available, and exchanged for the value of the precious metal they contained. Money was very rare and not in general circulation.

FRONTIER TRADE GOODS

Pocket knives
Pen knives
Butcher knives
Table knives
Skinning knives
Small metal tools
Awls
Augers
Rasp
Files
Chisels
Sugar nippers
Brass thimbles
Metal coat buttons
Axe heads
Cinnamon
Table knives and forks

Scutcheons—metal plates
Small or large saws
Thread, needles
Scissors—hand forged
Piloncillo—brown sugar
Cotton fabric—calico
Linen fabric
Buckles
Ink packets
Paper
Pipes
Slate
Playing cards
Brick tea from China
Triangular needles for sewing leather
Porta crayon—lead pencil

The Taos Mountain Trail was Well Traveled.

Denver Public Library

Taos was central to the mountain traders who traveled up the Taos Mountain Trail or over to the San Luis Valley. They bought trade goods, then sold their furs and buffalo robes in Taos. The *arrieros* or mule packers knew how to help the traders haul their goods on pack mules. A trader might have 20 mules and a number of arrieros with him when he went out to trade.

Robert W. Pacheco

Taos was home to people with many skills. A blacksmith was always in demand. The few pieces of metal available were shaped into spoons, plows, or tools by the blacksmith. The metal came from Mexico or was imported from the United States as scutcheons or fla plates of metal.

Tom Tobin came to Taos in 1837 at age 14. His half brother Charles Autobees was a trader and Tom traveled the trade route from Taos to Fort Jackson, to Bent's Fort and El Pueblo Trading Post. Tom delivered messages through dangerous country for the Americans and was well known as a tracker. His wife, Pascuala Bernal, and his family were important to him. He built them a home in Arroyo Hondo, eight miles north of Taos, were he worked at a distillery.

Charles Bent, an American, and Ceran St. Vrain, a Frenchman, opened a store in Taos in 1832. It was more profitable for one partner to manage the store while the other partner traveled the Santa Fe Trail to bring more goods to sell. Traders used these stores to stock up on goods to trade with the Native Americans for furs and other goods.

The ruling class families like the Chavezes and Pereas had homes built in the traditional style around a central square. The haciendas had rooms for the family members and their servants. When a family member married, often rooms were added to form a second square behind the first.

Doña María Gertrudis Barceló

Money was in very short supply to pay the Army of the West stationed in Santa Fe. Doña Gertrudis was a business woman operating a gambling parlor and saloon. She was one of the three women to trade on the Santa Fe Trail. She loaned the American army money to pay their soldiers in Santa Fe.

Mexican American War
1846-48

In September, 1846, Kearny marched into Santa Fe and took the city as a conquest of war without firing a single shot. Other generals marched south and conquered Mexico, even marching and battling in Mexico City. Kearny continued on to California, leaving Alexander Doniphan in charge. The people of Santa Fe and New Mexico were unsure about the benefits of becoming part of the United States.

Simeon Turley came to Taos in 1830, married Maria Rosita Vigil y Romero. He built a two-story mill in Arroyo Hondo. He grew wheat for flour but also to make a whiskey know as Taos Lightening. Traders bought Turley's whiskey for resale to the Native Americans. Turley employed Charles Autobees and Tom Tobin to trade for him. Turley often had an employee at El Pueblo Trading Post to sell trade goods and whiskey. The ten-gallon whiskey kegs were transported by burro across the Taos Mountain Trail.

Taos Insurrection
1846-48

After the Americans invaded the Mexican lands, Taos openly rebelled in January 1847. Native American people of Taos Pueblo and the Mexicans of Taos attacked and killed a number of Americans, including the American governor, several appointed government officials, and Simeon Turley. The American military and volunteers marched on Taos. They fought the resistors, defeating and capturing them. A court then convicted the men and hanged them as traitors to the new American government.

Visitors to Bent's Fort:

Cheyenne Chief Yellow Wolf

Arapaho Chief Left Hand

Cheyenne Chief Black Kettle

Comanche, Kiowa, and Ute groups

Col. John Charles Fremont

General Stephen W. Kearny

Susan and Sam Magoffin

Col. Alexander Doniphan

Arapaho Chief Little Raven

In 1830, American brothers Charles and William Bent partnered with Ceran St. Vrain to begin trade with Mexico. The United States government issued a trading license to Bent, St. Vrain & Company. The Bent brothers returned to Independence, Missouri in 1832 with $190,000 worth of mules, silver bullion and furs, according to one newspaper account. In 1833, the partners built a trading post on the Arkansas River.

Bent's Fort was located on a branch of the Santa Fe Trail between Independence, Missouri and Santa Fe, New Mexico Territory. The Fort was the largest structure of the time between Missouri and California. The *adobe* walls were 15 feet high and three feet thick.

Inside the gates, a central *placita*, or commons area, was surrounded by living quarters for the employees. Bent's Fort housed storage rooms, trade rooms, and workshops for blacksmiths, carpenters, and tailors. The Fort dining room was legendary for the formal meals served on china dishes.

Robert W. Pacheco

When Bent's Fort was built, 150 Taos men came to make the adobe bricks and raise the walls. The final coating of adobe had to be reapplied every year to keep it weatherproof. Women traditionally applied this final covering of adobe.

Trade items clockwise from top: grain measure, whip or quirt, wooden spoon, cup from buffalo horn.

Robert W. Pacheco

Native Americans came to Bent's Fort to trade hides for convenience goods such as kettles, Navajo blankets, needles, and fabric. They often camped near the trading post. William Bent also traded for horses and captives. Sometimes the Cheyenne would dance for visitors traveling the Santa Fe Trail.

Bent's Fort served trappers and traders, traveling on the Santa Fe Trail, and the Plains Native American groups. A big part of the trade was hides, pelts, and leather goods. Beaver hides, or plews, were so valuable that all the beaver on the Arkansas River had been trapped by 1821. The animals could still be found in northern Colorado. Traders traveled to South Platte or North Park, traded with the Nations wintering there, then traded the furs or plews back at Bent's Fort or Taos. Charles Bent took wagonloads of hides to St. Louis to sell.

Conestoga wagons held 1500 bulk weight units. One wagon hauled household goods for a family moving west or thousands of pounds of merchandise for the traders. Some wagons were so large that six or eight oxen were needed to pull them. Wagons traveled 12 to 15 miles per day.

BENT'S FORT

Trade goods included white, red, and blue beads, red cloth, brass wire, and hoop iron for making arrowheads. Knives and small axes also were good trade items. Abalone shells for making earbobs (earrings) for the warriors or decoration for clothing and dried vegetables were valuable trade goods.

The fur press was a box with a simple screw press used to compact 10 buffalo hides into 100-pound bales.

In 1842, Bent's Fort traded for 1,670 beaver plews valued at $7,836.12 and 3,000 buffalo robes valued at $7,535.80. These were transported by wagon back to St. Louis for sale.

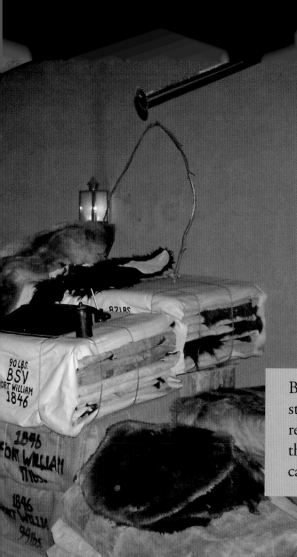

Storekeepers had to know how to read, write and do math. Accounts for each trader were written in a ledger. The traders also carried gifts for the chiefs of the village such as coffee and sugar for making "black soup." These items were packed in three-pint Connecticut clay cups.

Bales of buffalo robes and piles of furs were kept in the storerooms until ready to transport. Labels on the bales read "Fort William." Although the Bent brothers named their castle on the plains "Fort William," all the traders called it Bent's Fort.

Bent's Fort on the Santa Fe Trail saw heavy traffic. The table below shows the value of merchandise, the number of wagons and men compared to the number of owners. The last column shows the value of the merchandise transported through Santa Fe to Chihuahua.

Year	Value of Merchandise	Wagons	Men	Owners	Trade to Chihuahua
1834	$150,000	80	160	50	$70,000
1836	130,000	70	135	35	$60,000
1838	$90,000	50	1000	20	$40,000
1840	$50,000	30	60	5	$10,000
1842	$160,000	70	120	15	$90,000
1843	$450,000	230	350	30	$300,000

From Joshia Gregg's book Commerce of the Prairies (page 332)

Several loaded mules accompanied the trader. They used the standard pack saddle or the native pack basket. A mule weighing 700 pounds could carry 350 pounds of goods.

The success of Bent's Fort was due to the tireless work of many people. Charles Bent led caravans across the plains from St. Louis and back. William Bent spent much of his time trading with the Nations of the Plains. Ceran St. Vrain lived in Mora, NM, and tended to the demands of the store there. The daily operation of the Fort fell on the shoulders of Bent's trusted employees.

Two workers remove the fat and flesh from a beaver hide to prepare for the tanning process. Brains and liver were used for tanning. Beaver and buffalo were hunted in the winter when the fur was thick.

Year-round workers at Bent's Fort included the *vaqueros* or Mexican cowboys. Since there was little grass around the Fort, the herds had to be taken to other pastures to feed.

Children went barefooted or wore moccasins. Shoes made by a cobbler were an expensive import item from either St. Louis or Chihuahua.

ent's Fort employees included a French tailor from New Orleans, an Irishman who hauled water and trash, plus various housekeepers, cooks, hunters, bullwhackers, herdsmen, clerks, and caravan leaders. These employees lived at the Fort with their families who also worked. Craftsmen such as gunsmiths and wheelwrights were also employed. Andrew, Dick and Charlotte Green were slaves owned by the Bents. Andrew held a trader's license. They worked at the Fort until they were freed around 1849.

Gathering wood to keep the fires burning was a task for everyone. Buffalo chips (dried manure) were also gathered for fuel.

Capote coats were often made of wool blankets with the blanket colors on the sleeves. The wool *sarape*, a loose covering with an opening woven in the middle, kept children warm.

By 1840, half of all the wagons on the Santa Fe Trail traveled to Chihuahua, Mexico to trade. Many American merchants passed through Bent's Fort, staying for a night or a few days. Few Mexican traders going to the east stopped at Bent's.

William Bent married the daughter of Gray Thunder, keeper of the medicine arrows of the southern Cheyenne in1837. His relationship with the Cheyenne influenced his activities and Bent policies through his life. Bent's wife Mis-stan-stur, or Owl Woman, was accompanied by her sister Yellow Woman. William and Owl Woman had four children. When she died, Yellow Woman took over the Bent household and had one child with William.

Robert W. Pacheco

Resident blacksmiths kept the wagons in repair and did work for travelers who needed items made for the trail. Metal of all kinds was in short supply and was a trade item. The metal was often called scutcheons or flat rectangles of iron that the blacksmith formed into hinges, tools, metal parts for wagons.

Meals were simple. Workers were not invited to eat at "first table" with the chief traders and head clerks. The Mexican workers tended to small herds of milk cows, sheep, and goats used for food. Chickens, turkeys and pigeons lent variety to the food supply. Traders brought dried vegetables to the Fort.

The military used Bent's Fort as a stopping point. Stephen Watts Kearny passed through with his dragoons in 1835 on his way to California. John Fremont stopped by with a survey group. The United States declared war against Mexico on May 13, 1846. Supply trains and Stephen Watts Kearny's 1700 soldiers met at the Fort. Soldiers purchased items from the Bent store. Supplies ran short and tempers were shorter. Tents stretched for many miles along the Arkansas River. An estimated 20,000 horses, mules and oxen tried to find enough to eat on the bare prairie around the fort. Each week, 30 wagons of supplies were hauled to Santa Fe for the military. Nearly 140 tons of supplies were left at Bent's.

In 1846, Charles Bent was appointed the first American governor of the New Mexico region after Kearny's army invaded Santa Fe.

Bent's Fort Burns To The Ground

Bent, St. Vrain & Company became the only group of traders in a very large region. The company bought out competitors the American Fur Company and the Vasquez & Sublette Company. Bent, St. Vrain & Company either built or took over Fort St. Vrain, Fort Lupton, and Fort Adobe in Texas. William built another home at Big Timbers, thirty miles east of the first fort. Bent's new fort was not as large as the first fort.

In January 1847, patriots in Taos revolted and killed all Americans in town, including Charles Bent. William Bent and Ceran St. Vrain continued the businesses. St. Vrain wanted to sell Bent's Fort to the military but William was unhappy with the price offered. St. Vrain soon sold his share in Bent's Fort to William.

Owl Woman, William's wife, died in childbirth with their fourth child the same year.

Cholera struck the Plains and half of the Southern Cheyenne died. On August 21, 1849, William ordered his employees to pack up everything of value into 22 wagons. The wagons left for Big Timbers. The same day, Bent's Fort burned to the ground. The eastern wall had been shattered by kegs of gunpowder.

William Bent continued to trade with the Nations of Plains from Big Timbers and served as an Indian Agent.

A replica of Bent's Old Fort was built on the site of the Castle on the Plains. It was declared a National Historic Site in 1960 and became a National Park.

KEY ACTIVITIES

- Fitzpatrick's Indian Agency here
- US offers to buy Bent's Fort
- Charles Bent killed in Taos
- William refuses War Department offer
- Gold discovered Pikes Peak 1849
- Cholera kills thousands on the plains
- Half of the Southern Cheyenne die
- William Bent orders 22 wagons loaded
- Bent's Fort burns to the ground
- Fort St. Vrain rebuilt for trade

In 1842, a number of Americans set up a base camp for trade with the Nations of the Plains. They chose the north shore of the Arkansas River because it was far from the oversight of both Mexican and American governments. The Arkansas River was the border between Mexico and the United States.

They hired *adoberos* from Taos to build the trading post of adobe. The Americans soon brought their Native American or Spanish/Mexican wives and children to live at the trading post. The children provided an additional workforce. Simeon Turley from Taos kept a storekeeper at El Pueblo just to handle his goods.

Children at El Pueblo spent their days working. They hauled water from the river, cut firewood, and watered the rooftop gardens. Children helped to prepare meat or vegetables for drying to preserve food for the winter. They also helped bake bread in the big outdoor ovens called *hornos*.

From their base camp at El Pueblo, traders traveled with their *arrieros* and mules on expeditions up to the South Platte, North Park, or Rio Salado where the Nations camped. They crossed the Wet Mountains to places where bands of Utes often camped. Because the Native American villages were mobile, sometimes a trader would return without finding the group he was seeking.

To Denver

EL PUEBLO

BENT'S FORT

La Junta

Butte

Taos Trail

Huerfano River

Old Santa Fe Trail

Fort Garland

Trinidad

San Luis

COLORADO

NEW MEXICO

TAOS

Raton

Cimarron

Santa Fe

To Mexico

El Pueblo men also traveled north up to Wyoming to trade flour, grain, fabric, or other necessities with emigrants on the Oregon Trail. From these negotiations, traders returned to El Pueblo with dairy cattle. Sometimes the trader's Native American wife traveled with him, bringing her teepee and children.

Many women of El Pueblo remained behind while the men traveled for trading. The Spanish/Mexican women made clothing of fabric and knitted stockings. They made soap and candles if the men brought home tallow (buffalo fat). The Native American women made leather clothing and moccasins. They gathered and dried herbs for medicine and food.

Although there was no "store" at El Pueblo, the empty wooden boxes of guns might have been stacked to form a counter. The clerk wrote the goods traded and the number of hides or pelts received in a journal with his quill pen. Ink and paper were trade items but people made their own quill pens.

Hides of various animals:
Coyote, badger, raccoon, elk, buffalo

VALUE IN TRADE

ONE TANNED BUFFALO ROBE WAS WORTH:

- 1 common blanket
- 1 shirt
- 1/2 yard blue cloth
- 1/2 yard scarlet cloth
- 20 loads ammunition and 10 papers vermillion
- 20 loads ammunition and 1 knife
- 20 loads ammunition and bunch small beads

MUSKRAT OR MINK HIDES WERE WORTH:

- 2 flints
- 1 gun worm
- 1 awl
- 4 bells

12 beaver plew or buffalo robes for one rifle

James Beckwourth was a mountain man, trader and guide. He lived among the Crow people for many years. When he returned to Taos, he married Luisa Sandoval. In 1842 they moved to El Pueblo where Luisa gave birth to daughter Matilde. Beckwourth soon left on trading expeditions. He is credited with discovering Beckwourth Pass through the northern California mountains on the emigrant route of the Oregon Trail.

Robert W. Pacheco

Corn and chili were staples of the El Pueblo diet as well as trade items. During droughts, the Native Americans traded for corn to feed their horses as well as themselves. Wheat flour was a trade item brought from Taos and used to make both bread and *tortillas*. Other trade items brought to El Pueblo were *piloncillos*, or Mexican brown sugar cones, calico fabric, lye soap, needles, thread, and scissors.

Large frontier families meant that children at El Pueblo were half of the population. The main meal of the day could be a stew of dried meat and vegetables. A Dutch oven or a large clay bowl called a *cazuela* was placed in the middle of a buffalo robe and the diners dipped tortillas or bread into the pot. Individual spoons, plates or cups were not available as they were costly trade items. The men ate first, then, the women and children.

At the beginning of the 1800, there were about 11 million buffalo. By 1889, less than 1000 buffalo remained alive.

Grizzly bears, 7 feet tall and weighing 800 pounds, are a threatened species no longer living in Colorado or New Mexico.

Cats were a trade item. They helped to control the mouse population.

THE BUFFALO RANCH

When Matthew Kinkead moved to El Pueblo, buffalo were selling in Canada for $100 per head. He decided to build a ranch to raise buffalo, then herd the animals to Canada. With Teresita Sandoval's help, he gathered buffalo calves from the herds, planning to raise them on cow's milk. The cows had to be tied down to allow the buffalo calves to suckle. The ranch failed and Kinkead moved to California taking his son Andres with him.

Drying food was the only way to preserve meat or vegetables for the winter months. People also prepared dried vegetables for trade to the tribes. Children prepared small vegetables by stringing and hanging them to dry in the sun. Strips of meat dried on the roof of the trading post. A child looked after the drying and chased away birds or cats.

Teresita Sandoval remained at El Pueblo with Alexander Barclay, a corset maker from England. Barclay was a clerk at Bent's Fort before going out on his own as a trader. Teresita, son Tom Suaso (15), and baby Rafaela lived and worked at El Pueblo with Barclay. Teresita's daughters soon married American traders. Cruz, 13, married Joseph Doyle and Juana, 14, married George Simpson. When Juana and George had baby Isabel in 1844, the Native American women brought her many pairs of tiny, beaded moccasins as gifts.

Native American wives of traders lived in their own teepees near the trading post. Charles Autobees had both an Arapaho wife, Sycamore, and a Spanish/Mexican wife Maria Serafina Avila. Sycamore traveled with Autobees. Serafina lived in Taos. When Charles built a ranch nine miles south of El Pueblo, he built a home for Serafina and across the road, a home for Sycamore. The Autobees settlement was the first thriving farming community on the Arkansas.

No beaver lived on the Arkansas River by 1821 although they were still trapped in northern Colorado.

Coyotes, the scavengers of the prairie, had beautiful fur.

Hog's heads, five or ten gallon wooden kegs, held whiskey. Because alcohol was diluted for trade with the Native Americans, two-gallon kegs were often filled one-tenth of the way with pure grain alcohol. Water was added when the trader neared the location for trading. Smaller kegs were used for gunpowder. When sold, it was poured into the buyer's own powder horn.

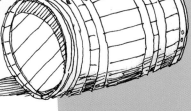

WHAT THEY WORE

All clothing was made by hand from available materials. A coyote fur might become a little girl's winter cape. Leather pants could be traded for an extra shirt of leather or calico. Shoes or boots had to be imported from Chihuahua, Mexico or from St. Louis as there were no cobblers at El Pueblo, Bent's Fort, or Taos.

Most people wore moccasins. A woman might have only two or three skirts (often worn at the same time for warmth), a couple of blouses, and a shawl or *reboso* in her wardrobe. Barclay made coats called capotes from woolen trade blankets.

Prairie dogs lived in colonies with as many 3000 animals. The black-tailed prairie dog is now endangered.

In 1846, a group of "Mississippi Saints" spent the winter at El Pueblo. They were traveling west to meet their leader, Brigham Young and other pioneers going west to California Territory. In July, they arrived at Fort Bernard near Fort Laramie, Wyoming. They were advised to go to El Pueblo to stay for the winter.

The Mormons were not welcome in the eastern states because of their religion, so they were traveling west to find a home free of persecution. Soon sick soldiers from the Mormon Battalion, who were serving in the United States Army, joined the families at El Pueblo. The population grew to nearly 350 people, 47 of them women and an unknown number of children.

One of the first cabins built in the row was a larger room used for church meetings, dances, and school. The people of El Pueblo Trading Post were invited to listen to church programs and stay for the dancing. During their stay at El Pueblo, the Mormons learned many skills that would be useful to build homes in the West. In the East, ditches were used to drain water away from the fields. At El Pueblo, irrigation ditches or *acequias* provided water for the fields.

The women learned how to bake bread in the *hornos* and how to survive the weather. For their sick and injured, the Mormons used Native American herbs or Mexican remedies. The men trained in blacksmithing did work at both El Pueblo and Bent's Fort. They worked so hard that when they left El Pueblo, they had 300 cattle and 100 horses. The Mormons also learned *abobe* skills so that the first building in Utah was of adobe. They also took with them the white Taos wheat that thrived in high altitude. They left in May 1847.

Mormon Town, with a couple rows of long, attached cabins, was built across the river and half a mile east of the trading post. Some of the men were blacksmiths and worked at either Bent's Fort or El Pueblo Trading Post doing various jobs.

Final Days of El Pueblo Trading Post

The Utes and Apaches were very upset with the Americans who did not keep a promise to protect native lands from invading settlers. At an 1854 a treaty council, the chiefs received soldier jackets as gifts for signing. The chiefs and their people became sick with smallpox and died. Nearly half of the 700 Moache Utes died from the disease. In revenge, the Utes attacked settlements in the Arkansas and San Luis Valleys.

On December 24, 1854, the chief Tierra Blanca and his band of Utes and Jicarilla Apaches attacked and killed everyone at El Pueblo Trading Post. Four of the Apaches and Utes also died. They captured two boys—Felix Sandoval, age 12, and his brother Juan Isidro, age seven, —and a woman, Chipeta Miera who soon died.

Felix was rescued eight months later when the Utes and Apaches asked for a peace council at Abiquiu, New Mexico. Juan Isidro had been traded to the Navajos. He lived with them for nearly 6 years. A Mexican trader saw him during a trade visit to the Navajo camp. He bought the boy and sold him back to his mother in Santa Fe for 300 silver dollars.

For 12 years, El Pueblo Trading Post offered a place to trade and a base camp for traveling traders and their families. The Cheyenne, Ute, Kiowa, and Arapaho often camped nearby and brought their valuable animal hides and beaded clothing to trade. After the 1854 attack, the post was deserted. Its adobe bricks were later used to build the new town of Pueblo. The *placita* and its outbuildings melted into the Colorado dirt and disappeared.

The Colorado Historical Society built an evocation of El Pueblo Trading Post in 1994. Dedicated historical interpreters bring the post to life for its annual Mercado.

1400 Tiwa Pueblo built.

1598 Fray Francisco de Zamora sent to Taos Pueblo.

1610 Spanish presidio at Santa Fe established.

1680 Pueblo Revolt—Spanish driven out of New Mexico.

1692 Return of the Spanish, new guidelines on relations with Native Americans.

1700s Apache forced from their hunting ground along the Arkansas by the Comanche.

1706 Spaniard Juan de Ulibarri visited the Rio Nepestle (Arkansas River).

1739-1752 Various traders reached Santa Fe; some arrested.

1776 First maps of northern New Mexico and central Colorado to headwaters of the Arkansas, and Platte by Dominguez/Escalante group.

1776 Census by Father Dominguez records 306 Spaniards in Taos Valley.

1779 Apache and Ute allies join Spanish Governor Juan Bautista de Anza to defeat the Comanche.

1792-93 Frenchman Pedro Vial explored the path between Santa Fe and St. Louis by order of New Spain's viceroy.

1803 Louisiana Purchase U.S. buys 828,800 square miles from France.

1804 New Spain arrests Baptiste La Lande for traveling to Santa Fe to trade.

1804 Trader Severino Martinez built Martinez Hacienda in Taos.

Denver Public Library

1804 Lewis and Clark leave to travel across new territories.

1806 Zebulon Pike, explorer, crosses into Spanish lands and is arrested by the Spanish.

1807 Missouri merchant Jacquez Clamorgan traveled to Santa Fe and down to Chihuahua to trade.

1810 Zebulon Pike publishes his book on travels in Colorado, New Mexico, Chihuahua, Texas, and to Louisiana.

1812 Seven men reach Santa Fe to trade but are arrested and remain in Spanish custody until 1821.

1820 Explorer American Stephen H. Long labels the lands on the Arkansas River as part of the Great American Desert.

1821 Mexico becomes free of Spanish control; Mexico allows foreign traders into its country.

1821 Santa Fe Trail opens.

1821 Samuel Adams Ruddock and William Becknell, on separate journeys. reach Santa Fe with a train of pack mules.

1822 Becknell returns to Santa Fe with wagons instead of pack mules.

1824 Mexican government issues ban on taking beaver in the northern provinces.

1825 Congress commissions a Survey of the Santa Fe Trail between Independence and Santa Fe.

1825 Signing of treaty with the Osage people at Council Grove providing peace for part of the Santa Fe Trail.

1826 Christopher 'Kit' Carson arrives in Santa Fe; William Bent arrives in Taos.

1828 Jim Beckwourth lived with the Crow in Wyoming/Montana.

1829 Tom Tobin works at Simeon Turley's general mercantile store.

1829 First ox drawn wagons used.

1834 First printing press brought from Mexico for use by Father Antonio Martinez at his school, prints first newspaper in the New Mexico territory.

1834 Bent's Fort completed.

1836 Charles Autobees sent to sell whiskey and trade goods to Native Americans on the Plains.

1836 Republic of Texas declares independence from Mexico.

1840 Half of all freight on the Santa Fe Trail continues on the Camino Real to Chihuahua, Mexico.

1841 Texas Republic's military expedition to add Santa Fe to Texas is defeated. The 300 Texans are marched to prison in Chihuahua.

1842 El Pueblo Trading Post built.

1843 Kincead Buffalo Ranch begins, then abandoned.

1845 Texas admitted to the United States although border with Mexico is disputed.

1846 Mexican-American War begins. Congress declares war May 13.

1846 Mormon soldiers winter at El Pueblo Trading Post.

1846 Col. Stephen Kearny captures Santa Fe with the Army of the West on August 19.

1847 Doña Gertrudís Barceló provides the money to pay American troops in Santa Fe.

1847 Insurrection in Taos results in death of Charles Bent first appointed American governor of New Mexican Territory.

1851 In treaty, Apaches given reservation near Abique, NM, then moved to Dulce Reservation in 1887.

1852 Fort Massachusetts built.

1853 Autobees and others build settlement in Arkansas Valley.

1854 El Pueblo Trading Post attacked by Moache Utes. All residents and four Native American killed.

1858 Colorado gold rush begins.

1859 Town of Pueblo begins.

1848 Treaty of Guadalupe Hidalgo signed to end Mexican-American war giving citizenship to all who remain after a year, excluding Native Americans.

1849 Half of Southern Cheyenne dead from cholera.

1849 Bent's Fort closed, then burned; burned building becomes a stage stop. Bent moves to Big Timbers.

1849 California Gold rush begins.

1850 New Mexico admitted as a Territory.

1851 Fort Union, NM, built, becomes main staging area for military.

RELIVE THE PAST

While these pages reveal the history of trade, they also show the dedication of living history interpreters. Historical interpreters at national historic sites take the stories of the place and make them come alive for visitors. Search on the Internet for "living history" to find groups and organizations in local areas to join.

BENT'S OLD FORT

Sophia Alvarez	Greg Holt
Henry Crawford	Paul Imhof
Ed Duncan	David London
Lara Erickson	Jim Sebastian
Joseph Fausto	Jimmy Shasteen
Will Gwaltney	Shela Thurston
Jim Harsh	Isabella Vigil
Don Headlee	Josepheine Vigil

EL PUEBLO TRADING POST:

Kenton Brooks
Jim Colson
James Dietz
Rebecca Dietz
Deborah Espinosa
Juan Espinosa
Dora Hyder
Margie Joseph
Juan Madril
Deborah Martinez
 Martinez
Ralph McPherson

Mrs. Isabel Ortiz
Cassidy Perea
Carol Pickerel
Sophia Quintana
Marley Quintana
Mandell Reliford
Carol Rivera
Erica Salazar
Chloe Shumard
Ron Steiger
Virginia Vigil
Halee Villareal

Native American

Carlson, Paul H. (1998). The Plains Indians. Texas A&M University Press, 1998.

Kaelin, Cellinda R. & the Pikes Peak Historical Society. (2008). American Indians of the Pikes Peak Region (Images of America Series). Charleston, SC: Arcadia Publishing.

Maxwell, James A. (Ed.). (1978). Reader's Digest America's Fascinating Indian Heritage. Pleasantville, NY: The Reader's Digest Association, Inc.

Taos

Cisneros, Jose. (1984). Riders Across the Centuries: Horsemen of the Spanish Borderlands. El Paso, TX: University of Texas at El Paso.

Weber, David J., Miller, Skip, and Richardson, Anthony. (1996). On the Edge of Empire: The Taos Hacienda of Los Martinez. Santa Fe, NM: Museum of New Mexico Press.

Bent's Old Fort

Lavender, David. (1954). Bent's Fort. Lincoln, NE: University of Nebraska Press.

El Pueblo Trading Post

Buckles, William G. (1998). The Search for El Pueblo: Through Pueblo to El Pueblo, An Archaeological Summary. Pueblo, CO: City of Pueblo.

Garcia Simms, Charlene. (1998). "El Pueblo 1854 Christmas Tragedy." Denver, CO: Hispanic Genealogical Society of Southern Colorado.

Hammond, G. P. (Ed.). (1976). The Adventures of Alexander Barclay Mountain Man. Denver, CO.

Lecompte, Janet. (1978). Pueblo, Hardscrabble, Greenhorn: Society on the High Plains, 1832-1856. Norman, OK: University of Oklahoma Press.

Wilson, Elinor.(1972). Jim Beckwourth-Black Mountain Man and War Chief of the Crows. Norman, OK: University of Oklahoma Press.

Children's Books:

American Girls Collection. (1999). Welcome to Josefina's World-1824. Chicago, IL: Pleasant Company.

American Girls Collection. (2003). Welcome to Kaya's World-1764. Chicago, IL: Pleasant Company.

Bacon, Melvin and Blegen, Daniel. (1995). Bent's Fort-Crossroads of Cultures on the Santa Fe Trail. Brookfield, CT: Millbrook Press.

Becker, Cynthia S. (2008). Chipeta: Ute Peacemaker. (Now You Know Bios Series). Palmer Lake, CO: Filter Press.

Bishop, Amanda, and Kalman, Bobbie. (2003). Life in a Pueblo. NY, NY: Crabtree Publishing Company.

Cheyenne-Arapaho Book Project. Hinono'ei Way of Life, Prairie Thunder People, Tsististas Journey, Tsististas: People of the Plains. Contact Funston Whiteman, Project Director, 405-213-5443.

Kalman, Bobbie. (2001). Life in a Plains Camp. NY, NY: Crabtree Publishing Company.

Kalman, Bobbie. (2001). Nations of the Plains. NY, NY: Crabtree Publishing Company.

Children's Fiction

Carson, William C. (2002). Peter Becomes a Trail Man. Illustrated by Pat Oliphant. Albuquerque, NM: University of New Mexico Press.

Finley, Mary Peace. (1999). Little Fox's Secret: The Mystery of Bent's Fort. Palmer Lake, CO: Filter Press.

WEBSITES:

El Pueblo History Museum
http://www.coloradohistory.org/hist_sites/Pueblo/Pueblo.htm

Bent's Old Fort National Historic Site (U.S. National Park Service)
http://www.nps.gov/beol/index.htm

Taos Historical Society
http://www.taos-history.org/

Martinez Hacienda
http://taosmuseums.org/hac_martinez.php

http://www.taoshistoricmuseums.org/hacienda-de-los-martinez/

Fur Trade History
www.thefurtrapper.com

Santa Fe Trail History
www.vlb.us/old_west/trails/sfthist.html

Taos Pueblo
www.taospueblo.com

Abalone California shellfish family Haliotidae

Adobe *Sp*, Mud and straw bricks

Adoberos *Sp*, Builders who use adobe bricks

Arrieros *Sp*, Mule packers and drovers

Bullwhackers Wagon drivers

Capote Long cape, usually with a hood

Carreta *Sp*, Two-wheeled cart with high sides

Cazuela *Sp*, Large clay bowl

Chili *Sp*, Hot green or red peppers

Cholera Intestinal disease

Cobbler Person whose work is making shoes

Dentalium Marine mollusk

Efectos de Pais *Sp*, Local trade goods

Evocation A recreation of the past

Genizaros *Sp*, Captured Native Americans raised by the Spanish

Hacienda *Sp*, Large ranch

Hogshead Large cask or barrel

Horno *Sp*, Outdoor adobe oven

Lye Soap Strong, abrasive solution of cleaners

Metate *Sp*, Grinding stone

Moccasins Shoes of leather

Obsidian Black volcanic glass

Parfleche *Fr*, Bag made of untanned animal hide

Piloncillo *Sp*, Brown cane sugar formed as a cone

Placita *Sp*, Interior square of a house

Plew Beaver skin, untanned

Porta Crayon *Fr*, Lead Pencil

Presidio *Sp*, Garrison or fort

Real *Sp*, Coin of New Spain, one dollar

Reboso *Sp*, Long, rectangular shawl

Rendezvous *Fr*, gathering or appointed meeting place

Replica Accurate reproduction of an object

Rescates *Sp*, Rescued people

Scutcheon Metal rectangle

Serapes *Sp*, Rectangular fabric with central hole for the head

Shinny A game played with a leather ball and curved sticks

Sinew Band of tissue attaching muscle to bone

Tallow Hard, fat from sheep or cattle, to make candles, soap

Tiwa Language of the Taos Pueblo people

Tortilla *Sp*, Round, unleavened bread

Travois *Fr*, Sled of two poles joined by a frame pulled by an animal

Vaqueros *Sp*, Mexican cowboys

Vermillion Bright red pigment from mercuric sulfide

Yucca Evergreen plant with sharp lance-shaped leaves

Sp=Spanish word   *Fr*=French word

45

VANISHING HORIZONS
PUBLISHING THE PAST FOR THE FUTURE

Many thanks to the historical interpreters, and especially Barbara Ingles.

© 2010 Deborah Martinez Martinez and Robert W. Pacheco, Illustrator

Art Director:	Robert W. Pacheco
Computer Graphic Design:	Kent Jodrie
Book Design:	Robert W. Pacheco & Kent Jodrie
Published by:	Vanishing Horizons, ~~PO Box 2118~~, Pueblo, CO 81004
	www.vanishinghorizons.com

Library of Congress Control Number:	2010930860
Martinez Martinez, Deborah and Pacheco, Robert W.	Trade on the Taos Mountain Trail, history, illustration, photos 1. Trade--History of trade 2. Colorado/New Mexico National Historic Sites 3. Southwestern US 4. Historiography
Cover Art and Design:	© by Robert W. Pacheco All illustrations not otherwise designated © by Robert W. Pacheco
Historical Photographs and Illustrations:	Denver Public Library, Western History Collection: Painted Buffalo Hide, 8, Chief's robe, Minitari Hidatsa, Collected by Maximilian Prince of Wied from the upper Missouri riverbanks around 1844, X-32482, pg. 8; Taos Trail ("View of Sangre de Cristo Pass), sketch by Richard Kern, 1853, for E.G. Beckwith's Pacific Railway Survey Report, F-38058, pg. 19; Unidentified Comanche group, photographer unknown, X-32213, pg. 1, 38; Unknown woman and child, Cheyenne, photographer unknown, X-33853, pg. 5; "Plains Indian Family Moves," artist unknown, photographic reproduction of illustration, X-33702, pg. 2; "A Cheyenne Camp" by Fredrick Remington, 1889, magazine illustration, X-33774 (formerly F40780), pg. 2; "Starting Out as Trapper and Trader" from H.L. Conrad "Uncle Dick Wootten," F20999, pg.15.
Photographs:	Courtesy of Barbara Ingles (inglesb@centurytel.net), 8, 12, 13, 18, 19, 20, 23, 24, 25, 26, 27, 28, 29; Robert W. Pacheco, 17, 18, 23, 35, 42, 43; Carol Rivera, 17, 24; Glori Hyder, 31, 36, 39, 43; Pat Fox, 42; Sherri Grogan, 39.
Illustrations:	Courtesy of Douglas S. Candelaria (dcandelaria88@msn.com), 7, 10, 20, 37; Estate of Michael D. Martinez, 5, 11, 20, 21.

Printed in China by BookMasters, Inc. Kowloon, Hong Kong.
Printed August, 2010. Reference Number A22. Age group—9-10 years.